our wonderful
weather

valerie bodden

clouds

CREATIVE
PAPERBACKS

our wonderful
weather

Published by Creative Paperbacks
P.O. Box 227, Mankato, Minnesota 56002
Creative Paperbacks is an imprint of The Creative Company
www.thecreativecompany.us

Design and production by Christine Vanderbeek
Art direction by Rita Marshall
Printed by Corporate Graphics in the United States of America

Photographs by Alamy (J Marshall-Tribaleye Images, Marvin Dembinsky Photo
Associates), Corbis (Jim Reed Photography, Momatiuk-Eastcott, Eric Nguyen,
Erik Rank, Visuals Unlimited, Staffan Widstrand), Dreamstime (Greg Blomberg,
Pictureone.net), Getty Images (Eightfish, Johner, Frank Oberle, PhotoAlto/Laurence
Mouton, Steve Taylor, Travel Ink), iStockphoto (Ken Babione, Glenn Culbertson,
Martin Fischer, Uwe Loescher, Patrick Oberem, Cindy Singleton, Olada, Skyhobo,
vm, Ingmar Wesemann, Peter Zelei)

Library of Congress Cataloging-in-Publication Data

Bodden, Valerie.
Clouds / by Valerie Bodden.
Summary: A simple exploration of clouds, examining how these large masses of water vapor
develop, the different forms they take at varying altitudes, and the problems clouds can cause.
Includes bibliographical references and index.
ISBN 978-1-60818-146-9 (hardcover)
ISBN 978-0-89812-919-9 (pbk)
1. Clouds—Juvenile literature. I. Title.
QC921.35.B63 2012
551.57'6—dc22   2010052761

CPSIA: 030111 PO1449

First edition
2 4 6 8 9 7 5 3 1

contents

As the warm air rises, it gets cooler. Some of the water vapor changes into water or ice. The water and ice latch

onto tiny pieces of dust in the air and swirl together to make a cloud. The wind blows clouds across the sky.

Clouds look soft. But if you could touch clouds, they would feel wet! The highest clouds would feel very cold.

The biggest, thickest clouds have a lot of water in them

There are almost 100 different kinds of clouds.

Cirrus (SEER-us) clouds look like long, white streaks.

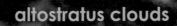

altostratus clouds

Altostratus (AL-toh-STRA-tus) clouds are blue or grayish clouds that can cover the whole sky.

Low, white, puffy clouds are called cumulus (KYOO-myoo-lus). Sometimes cumulus clouds grow very tall, with a wide,

cumulus clouds

flat top. Then they are called cumulonimbus (KYOO-myoo-loh-NIM-bus) clouds. These clouds make thunderstorms.

thunderstorm

13

Meteorologists (mee-tee-uh-RAH-luh-jists) are people who study weather. They try to forecast how the weather will change. They study clouds with radar and satellites. Clouds help tell them what kind of weather is coming.

Meteorologists may use big balloons to help study weather

15

Sometimes there are not enough clouds. It does not rain for a long time. This is called a drought (DROWT). In the 1930s, a huge drought dried up the land in the middle of the United States. The plants in farmers' fields died, and wind blew dust and dirt everywhere.

This farm in Texas was ruined by the drought in the 1930s

16

Clouds can bring too much rain and cause floods. They can cause other problems, too. Fog is a cloud that forms close to the ground. It can make it hard for people to see

flood

where they are going. Sometimes, in big cities, smoke mixes with fog to make smog. Smog is like dirty air. It can hurt the people who breathe it.

smog

We need clouds. They bring rain that waters plants and fills streams. Watching clouds can be fun, too. If you see a storm cloud coming, go inside! But if there are a few fluffy clouds in the sky, watch them spin into new shapes!

MAKE YOUR OWN CLOUD

You can see how a cloud forms by placing cold temperatures above warm water. First, fill a metal pie pan with ice cubes. Then, have a grown-up fill a glass jar with very hot water. Leave the water in the jar for about 10 seconds and then pour it out. Set the pie pan on top of the empty jar. Look carefully, and you will see a cloud form!

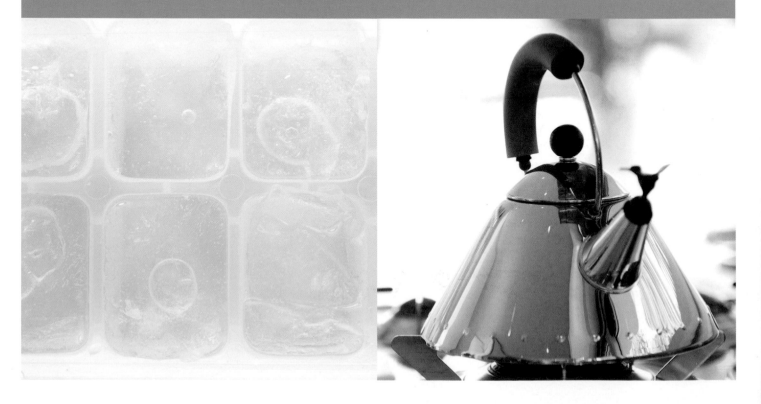

GLOSSARY

floods — large amounts of water that cover land that is usually dry

forecast — to try to figure out what is going to happen in the future, such as during the next day or week

ice crystals — tiny pieces of ice that have six sides and make snowflakes when they join together

radar — a system that uses radio waves and computers to measure how far away something (such as a cloud or thunderstorm) is and how fast it is moving

satellites — machines that circle Earth in space; weather satellites can takes pictures of clouds and measure temperatures

water vapor — water that has turned into drops so tiny that it rises into the air and becomes invisible

READ MORE

Harris, Caroline. *Science Kids: Weather*. London: Kingfisher, 2009.

Herriges, Ann. *Clouds*. Minneapolis: Bellwether Media, 2007.

WEB SITES

Kids Fun Online: Interactive Weather Maker

http://www.scholastic.com/kids/weather
Change the temperature to change the weather from sunny to cloudy or stormy.

Web Weather for Kids: Cloud Types

http://eo.ucar.edu/webweather/cloud3.html
See pictures of the different cloud types and play a cloud matching game.

INDEX